Riding the Waves of Bliss

Riding the Waves of Bliss

Seasons of Life Poems

SHAI HAR-EL

Homestead Lighthouse Press
Grants Pass, Oregon

The Tree of Life

In my heart, I planted a magnificent garden
to house my burning love, and there,
in this blossoming paradise,
I found a merciful and forgiving God.

I did not stop plowing, sowing,
bowing down, and kneeling,
worshiping Him one furrow after another,
even giving Him sacrifices and offerings.

Now its roots are spreading deep in my heart,
feeding fortitude to my trunk of faith,
inviting its crowning branches to cover my universe,
and its hanging fruits to sweeten my meditation.

Riding the Waves of Bliss Copyright © 2020 by Shai Har-El. All rights reserved. No part of this book may be reproduced or transmitted in any form without the prior written permission of the publisher.

ISBN 978-1-950475-08-7

Homestead Lighthouse Press
1668 NE Foothill Boulevard
Unit A
Grants Pass, OR 97526
www.homesteadlighthousepress.com

Distributed by Homestead Lighthouse Press, Amazon.com, Barnes & Noble, Daedalus Distribution.

Homestead Lighthouse Press gratefully acknowledges the generous support of its readers and patrons.

Book design by Ray Rhamey

I dedicate this poetry book to my children
Riv and James, Saritte and Etai, Natalie and David

Even if I am unheard
I know for certain
You are my living poems
Walking your own paths
Carrying my voice

CONTENTS

Preface / vii

PROLOGUE / 1

I Want to Write / 3

YEARNING and LONGING

Sailing Off into Yesterday / 6
On Yearning / 7
The Village Doesn't Live Here Anymore / 8
Travels through Time / 9
Once I was a Bird / 10
An Old Song in My Heart / 11
Childhood Memories / 13
Take Me Back Home Again / 15
To Love Israel / 16
A Family Tree / 18
Our Old House / 20
A Little Dream / 21
The Hill of Colors / 22

LOVE and INTIMACY

On Love / 26
A Destined Reunion / 28
Never Saw a Girl Like Her / 29
"Where Are You Running?" / 30

The First Kiss / 31
Secret Love / 34
A Vow / 35
A Lamentation on Love / 37
Memories of Separation / 38
Tour of the Heart / 39
Words of Love / 41
Aging Gracefully / 42
You Are Beautiful and You Are Mine / 43
Were It Not for You / 44
Riding the Waves of Bliss / 45
The Sculpture and the Lover / 47
Streams of Love / 49
I Want to Stay Inside You / 50
To Kiss You / 51
Heavenly Union / 53
My Perfect Ten / 54
A Song to My Beloved / 57
The Kiss of Life / 60

ONENESS and HARMONY

As Above, So Below / 64
Truth / 66
Peace / 67
Yes, I have a dream / 68
Brothers-in-Arms / 69
  You and I: A Quadrilogy on Oneness / 70
      a. Transcending Separation / 71
      b. A Flower of Being / 72
      c. A House of Worship / 73
      d. In the Heart of Hearts / 74

AWAKENING and ILLUMINATION

Transcendental Visions / 78
Seeking Illumination / 80
Discourse of Souls / 81
Soul Visions / 83
Always a Child / 85
Stages of Life / 86
Out of Jail / 88
The Invisible Mirror / 90
Riding to Nowhere / 92
The Tree of Life / 93
What is God? / 94
Where are You, God? / 95
Our Life / 97
Direct Line to Heaven / 98
God Must Have Had a Plan / 100
On the Top of Mount God / 102

DEATH and GRIEVING

A Hidden Visitor / 106
My Funeral Cry / 108
Three Goddesses of Destiny / 109
Visiting the Cemetery / 110
To Life or Death / 111
Life after death / 112
I am a Holocaust Survivor / 113
Elegy to Shmulik / 115
Mother, Don't Cry / 117
Change of Address / 119
A Wandering Spirit / 120

Nightmare / 121
Death of a Flower / 123
Every Person Finds for Himself a Flower / 124
On My Tombstone / 125

EPILOGUE

I am a Poet / 131

About the Author / 133

Preface

To everything there is a season,
        and a time to every purpose under the heaven:
a time to be born and a time to die,
a time to plant and a time to uproot,
a time to kill and a time to heal,
a time to tear down and a time to build,
a time to weep and a time to laugh,
a time to mourn and a time to dance,
a time to scatter stones and a time to gather them,
a time to embrace and a time to refrain,
a time to search and a time to give up,
a time to keep and a time to throw away,
a time to tear and a time to mend,
a time to be silent and a time to speak,
a time to love and a time to hate,
a time for war and a time for peace.
(Ecclesiastes 3:1-8)

As an epigraph to open my poetry book, I chose King Solomon's famous words of wisdom from the Book of Ecclesiastes (*Kohelet*, in Hebrew), as they represent the essence of my poetry—Seasons change so does human life.

    This collection of poetry is the story of my life. It serves as a splendid way for me to welcome you into my inner world, into my private exploration of my four landscapes of being—body, heart, mind, and spirit. Each poem is a window into my soul, an insight into the changing seasons of my life.

The Greek philosopher Aristotle distinguishes between two disciplines, history and poetry. He suggests that history reports what happened and therefore is concerned with particulars, whereas poetry is more philosophical and concerned with universals. I agree. My poetry is an authentic presentation of my inner world, and unlike history, the study of which I have been dedicating my life for many years, it is not subject to all the constraints and imperfections of actual life. I believe my poems, though autobiographical and personal, can appeal to anyone; the personal story in my poetry may illuminate your story because it tells the truth, my truth and yours. I described this kind of truth in one of my poems, portraying it *"like a petalled rose emerging from one stem offering its sweet fragrance and infinite beauty to humanity."*

With age come better knowledge and a wider experience of life. This comes up through my poems. Walking you through the seasons of my life, they start with a deep yearning and longing to the beginning, growing up in Israel; they continue through the experience of my multi-faceted love for and intimacy with my beloved wife, Rosie of blessed memory, the central figure in my life over 50 years; they shift to my preoccupation with the questions of oneness and harmony in the world; they go through the period of my spiritual awakening and illumination; and they finally end where life in This World concludes, in death and grieving.

Many of the poems in the last section were taken from A Psalm to Samuel (*Mizmor Li-Shmuel*, in Hebrew), a collection dedicated to my deceased brother, Shmulik. The actual writing of these poems was a cathartic experience that served as a catalyst to writing poetry. In my eulogy to my brother, I said *"you shined upon my way with your death,"* meaning that, with his demise, his image became a candle to light my life path.

Tragedies, like other life events, are our teachers. In the case of my brother's death, the birth of my poetry was a blessing in the curse.

I owe special thanks to my poetry mentor and editor, Robert McDowell, for his invaluable contribution to the final version of my book. Most importantly, I bow deeply out of gratitude to my deceased wife, Rosie of blessed memory, who had faithfully supported me and lived with this poetry anthology for many years.

I am dedicating my poetry collection in this book to my children, the best "investment" Rosie and I have ever made. Their contribution to our lives is invaluable. Not only did they give birth to eleven beautiful and smart grandchildren, they taught us what parenthood and loving care are all about.

Shai Har-El
Highland Park, Illinois
2020

PROLOGUE

I Want to Write

I want to write
I want to write the poems of my life
I want to cast simple ideas into illuminating structures
I want to cloth lost souls with literary garments
I want to light up dark places with gems of expression
I want to invite words and verses to live in a brilliant world
of
rhythm and music

YEARNING and LONGING

Sailing Off into Yesterday

Today,
My life boat is anchoring in tranquil waters.
The life that has passed is clearly reflected on the surface.
And the longing for yesterday
Is flooding my heart like sea waves.

Tomorrow,
My boat will be sailing into the open sea
With pictures, memorabilia, little stories,
And a map of memories
Back to the days of old that have gone forever.

On Yearning

I am in a desperate search
for a lost paradise. Although I arrived
in the "promised land," I dream of returning

to it, as if I never arrived there at all.
I long for the beginning,
wanting to feel the one moment before,

to return back into the womb,
into a tranquil and sweet place, into the mythic
"land flowing with milk and honey."

As I progress with age, and
the "black frame" of my death announcement zooms in,
a deep urge to return to point zero drives me.

As the future seems to get shorter and uncertain,
I look back more and more,
yearning for a distant past,

for the days of my childhood,
somewhere beyond the fog of time. And when I
finally arrive at my old home, and close a circle,

I find out, to my disappointment, that it
does not match the house of my childhood,
and I can never return to it again, never!

The Village Doesn't Live Here Anymore
(In memory of Rishon le-Zion, my old hometown in Israel)

My soul is grieving
    For the green fields of yesterday,
Buried under colossal buildings and traverse highways,
    Along with the footprints of my splendid childhood,
Entombing memories from another time.

The village doesn't live here anymore;
    Singing birds have flown away,
Wild pigeons have disappeared,
    Dancing butterflies have vanished,
Bleating sheep have left without saying goodbye.

The village doesn't live here anymore;
    The Community Center is silent,
Rothschild Avenue stands bashfully,
    Moishe Doodle with his newspapers has disappeared,
So has the innocence of my youth.

Travels through Time

I used to dream of myself
    Young and adventurous,
    Eager to discover vanished worlds
    Taking solo field trips
    Traveling in time back into distant pasts.

My little hands would easily dig a hole
    Deep into the belly of the earth
    Down into the unknown
    Suddenly falling into an unfamiliar time of antiquity
    Landing safely in the middle of an ancient metropolis.

An invisible visitor from an advanced civilization
    I was strolling the narrow streets,
    Watching open storefronts where merchants
    Dressed in medieval cotton flannel cloaks
    Were haggling in a strange Semitic tongue.

With a shepherd stick in my hand
    and a leather bag on my shoulder, I melded
    With the trafficking crowds in the central square
    Where all business dealings were conducted
    Taking notes to bring back home.

Once I was a Bird

Once I was a bird.

I always succeeded
In spreading my wings
Flying high in the sky
Gliding like a bird through the clouds
Circling over villages and fields
Watching people below waving to me.

Once I was a bird.

Today, I am sitting with my wings cut off
At the window sill
Looking far at my life horizon
Daydreaming of flying again
Soaring high like an eagle
Traveling to the end of the world.

An Old Song in My Heart

I have an old song in my heart
About days of gladness and pain
Of many 'once upon a time' stories
When our way of life was meaningful.

    Its melody feeds my soul
    It stimulates my longing.

I have an old song in my heart
About a warm and serene home
With a goodhearted and loving mother
And a father who cared above and beyond.

I have an old song in my heart
About a tiny and sweet room
Where we all together
Celebrated and sang.

I have an old song in my heart
About a smiling and loving grandfather
Who reminded me of holidays and festivals
And of keeping traditions and laws.

I have an old song in my heart
About a lost and vanished world
About a generation that has gone forever
From which no one survived.

    Its melody feeds my soul
    It stimulates my longing.

Childhood Memories
(Dedicated to my deceased brother, Shmulik)

Today, when I shed tears
Over your untimely death,
I remember you, my brother,
And will never stop telling.

I will tell about your birth day,
About the surprise that dropped upon me,
And the welcoming reception I prepared for you,
When I hid you twice in the drawer.

I will tell about the difficult recession,
When scarcity was everywhere,
When we went to the fields to gather manure,
To fertilize our vegetable garden.

I will tell about fields and orchards
That surrounded our house,
Where we leaped together catching butterflies,
Collecting insects and all kinds of creatures.

I will tell about the giant water tower,
Soaring in the outskirts of our neighborhood,
Which every child climbed,
And risked jumping off.

I will tell about the rare fruit trees,
The wild berries and the sugarcanes we chewed,
And the thorny cactus,
Whose seedy fruit we gobbled lustily.

I will tell about the wild yellow groundsels and red tulips,
We used to tie and interlace for a wreath,
And the sour wood-sorrels and herbal seeds.
In which our thrilled souls would delight.

Take Me Back Home Again

Take me back home again
To the wild days of youth
When I knew so well
How to climb tall trees
Without fear of falling.

Take me back home again
To the old days of innocence
When nothing prevented me
From chasing after butterflies
In the green fields of yesterday.

Take me back home again
To see the old world again
When life was so simple
Having so much fun and laughter
Seeking heart-pounding adventures nearby.

Take me back home again
Just one time.

To Love Israel

        To love Israel
is to retain
an emotional umbilical cord
to my birthing womb,
where God gifted me
His sacred soul,
breathed it into
my created flesh
and made me
a human being.

        To love Israel
is to always come back
with a great joy
to my ancestral home,
where I and an unbroken
chain of forefathers
have been drawn to
breathe its enchanting air
touch its antiquated soil
building there a place of our own.

To love Israel
is to be struck by an
unrestrained urge to belong
to my place of origin,
where relationships
are deeply rooted,
where memories
are constantly triggered,
particularly by the fragrance
of my mother's kitchen.

A Family Tree

From all aphorisms of nature
I see you as a huge oak tree
Blossoming through all seasons
Withstanding the cold and heat.

With a solid trunk, you are
Rooted deep into the earth
Fed by rich iron of strength
And fresh living waters.

You are proudly standing tall
Living among the lofty clouds
Nourished daily by the sun
And by night the radiant stars.

Your heavy branches extend far
Reaching outward in space
Growing the fruits of your heart
Under the shades of layers of leaves.

But to be a genuine tree
You cannot live apart
From the surrounding nature
That nurtures you.

You are a connected tree
Belonging to an extended family
Of trees whose thick roots
Are intertwined forever.

Our Old House

Was not just a house,
Not just a structure made of wood and stone,
But a dwelling cemented by love and devotion
A timeless place of family memories
With stucco walls that recall the sounds of laughter and cries
With wooden floors that hold the echoes of happy gatherings
A warm nest of boundless caring
Of children that blossomed like flowers of joy,
Growing up, marrying, and birthing their own fruits of love.

When the house was sold
And remained desolate of its inhabitants
I felt enormous guilt.
And when it was torn down
Erased from the face of the earth
My heart was broken.
My aching soul felt
The spirit of our house in pain
Unwilling to depart.

A Little Dream

The curtain rises
and they are all there,

taking their places
on the stage of life, and I,

an invisible visitor from heaven,
am sitting in the audience,

watching my eleven adult grandchildren
with pride and longing,

as they each play
their own role on planet earth.

The Hill of Colors

Every summer, the Hill of Colors, a natural
elevation rising on the outskirts of my old
neighborhood, was draped by a God-made

embroidery of red tulips, yellow marigolds
and other seasonal flowers. This preserved
hideaway has drawn young lovers from everywhere.

Today the Hill has been erased
from the face of the earth, becoming
an unnoticed island of wild weeds.

My first love brewed and fermented on
the Hill of Colors, infused forever
by the sweetness of a ripe watermelon

offered by a passing hiker, who
embarrassedly caught us by surprise
as we were sharing our new and ardent love.

LOVE and INTIMACY

On Love

Love is physical –
    passionate union of the flesh
    carnal urge that drives to connect
    deep thrust that wants to merge
    miraculous synthesis that creates matter
    powerful kiss that ignites fire
    vigorous force that stimulates water

Love is sensuous –
    endless pursuit of beauty
    aromatic smell of a red rose
    distinctive taste of a sweet cherry
    shivering touch of smooth velvet
    intuitive hearing of a heart's cry
    perceptive sight of a magnificent view

Love is spiritual –
    mystic meeting of two souls
    mercury-like fusion of two beings
    flow of energy between two heart fountains
    replacement of duality with unison
    merger of two lights into a single flame
    transformation of two opposites into one

Love is eternal –
> sacred covenant that binds spirited beings
> timeless bond that stands the seasons of life
> open space that allows coexistence to blossom
> continual link that ties the past with the future
> divine experience that transcends all barriers
> boundless universe that joins humanity together

A Destined Reunion

It all began
One wondrous evening
When twin souls
Longing to unite
Powerfully collided
Like guided meteors in the sky
On the way to their destined reunion
In the Garden of Eden on earth
Igniting a fire of love
That illuminated the sky
With a gallery of colors
Forming a brilliant rainbow bridge
Where our souls, hers and mine, met again
And joined in a holy covenant
Under the watchful eyes of God.

Never Saw a Girl Like Her

I came to welcome a cousin
Haven't seen before
What wholesome appeal
Sweet beauty of innocence
None like her among the girls.

She sprang forward
Like a dancing butterfly
Laying gently her wings upon me
Gracefully kissing my cheek
Never saw a girl like her.

Her glowing angelic eyes
Radiated lights of destiny
Her winning smile sending
Spellbinding beams of love
Conquering my heart forever.

"Where Are You Running?"

I just got to meet her
And I realized
That she walks fast
And although she stepped ahead
I enjoyed the charm of her movement.

"Where are you running?"
I asked politely.
"Please decelerate!"
I requested using a technical term
I learned in school.

"Is it because of light-mindedness
That she turns to me her back
Or because of body-lightness
That she quickens her steps?"
I watched in wonder.

Still today
After so many years
She walks swiftly ahead of me
As if she is in a hurry
To arrive first at our bed of love.

The First Kiss

An Israeli summer night in nineteen-sixty-six –
the Goddess of Love and the Lord of the Sea
sprang from the foam of the Mediterranean
to entice us to the Daughter of the Sea Beach.

Lovers are often drawn by the magic of
the sounding sea, the intoxicating scent in the air,
the slushy sands of the shore, an ideal electric
field for sparks that ignite two lonely hearts.

It was in the noon of night,
when Rosie and I headed to the beach
unaware that destiny
had already been decided in Heaven.

The deserted beach was lit
by a full yellow moon,
a sign of infinite possibilities
for a young couple yearning to connect.

We laid on a large towel for two
my body was close to her trembling body
and nothing in between but silence
the calm before a storm.

We watched the smiling moon with
a host of glittering stars throwing a show
turning their lights in our honor
to celebrate the initial burst of our love.

We listened to the sounds of the splashing
waves riding with the tides
swinging back and forth like
a repetitive mantra for meditators.

Immersed in the sea sounds
I felt heat wavelets and blood tides
flushing through my body.
My entire world overflowing.

"May I kiss you?" I requested.
and her hungry eyes closed down
as if her heart invited my heart
to take the first step.

No more words were necessary
for our lips to join in the first kiss,
sip together from the divine cup of love,
allowing our two halves to merge into a whole.

Years later, Rosie and I sat on the veranda
in the house we built on the hill
overseeing the Daughter of the Sea Beach,
where we first expressed our love.

We continued to listen to the sea waves,
praying to the Goddess of Love
and the Lord of the Sea
to protect us.

Secret Love

We were standing in a total embrace, you and I,
In the middle of the Jezreel Valley
In front of the sign "Entrance to the Ein Harod Spring."

The sun already set
But not our young love
That had just begun to rise.

We stood silently and stared at each other
Before we entered the nearby inn
To spend the first night of our secret love.

We were distant from everybody
Only the sky above was there to ask
"How long will you hide your love?"

We looked forward to another day of hiding
To taste together
The flavor of a sweet and forbidden fruit.

A Vow

*(Dedicated to the first ring, mounted with the Loving Cup,
I gave Rosie, when we first met)*

I offer you love;
for love is a rose
like the lips of beauty.

I offer you laughter;
for laughter is joy
like the song of birds.

I offer you support;
for support is strength
like the mountain's rock.

I offer you peace;
for peace is unity
like the earth joining the sky.

I offer you kindness;
for kindness is heartfelt warmth
like the sunshine kissing the blossom.

I offer you inspiration;
for inspiration is exhilaration
like stars that glitter the heavens high.

All I ask
in return
is
for you
to love me
for who I am
for through your love
I will receive from you all that I offer.

A Lamentation on Love

You have been for me
Like a rose among thorns
Scenting and sweetening my whole world.
But our love lost its fragrance,
Its vitality, perhaps its life.
The petals that shielded our love dried up
Slowly dropping from your hands.
The smiling rose has gone
The stinging thorn remained.
As if your sharp pricks
Were meant to wake me up
From a deep sleep.

Memories of Separation

I remember the separation like it was yesterday;
You said "it would only take a short time,"
But it turned into a lengthy year;
I beseeched you not to keep our souls apart,
When God joined them together;
Loving is following the heart where the fire was ignited;
But like a bird you were seeking to be free,
And so I remained grieving within my cage;
Our home became ruined and desolate,
A terrible sadness and fear of tomorrow engulfed me;
I did not stop missing your shining light,
Your sweet smile and angelic grace;
How could I ever replace, I feared,
The pleasure of your warm bosom?
Would I ever enjoy, I thought, such gentleness,
As I had seen in your soft face?
Would I ever find pleasure from a tender hand like yours,
That would caress my hair?
Will I ever know a different love?
To whom will I hand over the ring
You had placed on my finger?
I wanted you back so we could keep our vow;
The promise to live together without pause or boundary;
People whispered it was doomed to die,
Too many hurdles to overcome;
Indeed my eyes grew dark but in my heart I kept the light.

Tour of the Heart

You are invited
To visit my heart
And take a tour of
My sanctuary of love.

You will see a beautiful rose
Filling the entire chamber
With petals that change colors
Every season.

You will see a huge quilt
Of multicolored pieces
And different fabrics and patterns
Representing our diverse lives.

You will see a golden cup
Full of tears of joy
Collected drop by drop
Over many years.

You will see many tiny pictures
Hanging down from the ceiling
Showing our smiling faces
From past to present.

You will see a copper fireside
The seat of my soul
Radiating passionate love
Upon the blossoming rose.

Words of Love

Like a golden treasure,
Words of love,
The language of my heart,
Sit very deep inside
The fountain of my soul
Uneasily rising up
To the surface.

It takes a sacred moment,
My precious flower,
When your love embraces my love
And they stir together the water
Deep in the fountain of my soul
That the words arise like bubbles
And fill up my heart.

It takes a moment of truth,
My dear angel,
When I see the light of love
Deep inside your eyes
Wanting to burst out,
That words of love
Become a voice in my heart.

Aging Gracefully

Like dry flowers in the vase
Showing no freshness or vitality
You believe life reached its phase
Of worthlessness and human vanity.

Oh life is notably strange
A mix of cries and laughter
You hope the mirrors will change
When looking before and after.

You wonder if man
His youth can he save
Though life has its span
Between the cradle and the grave.

Life has no place to hide
To pretend, or to escape
What matters is the spirit inside
Not a form or shape.

Like a living flower, dearest wife,
You possess beauty and light
In all changing seasons of life
Even in the darkness of the night.

You Are Beautiful and You Are Mine

Love has nothing to do with age.
    Your hair quickly turns gray.
    Your skin may be slightly wrinkled.
    Your body is not what it used to be.

So is mine.
    You always tell me the older I get
    The more handsome I become.
    I feel the same way towards you.

Loving you leaves no place for ill-looking.
    It sees your gray hair as golden silk.
    It feels your aging skin as soft velvet.
    What I find in you is a flawless beauty.

Love endures beyond time or space.
    It listens to the echoes of the soul.
    It hears the whispers of the heart.
    What I see is what my soul and heart know.

You are beautiful and you are mine.

Were It Not for You

Were it not for you,
I would not be who I am today –
    A blend of heaven and earth,
        A man of soaring spirit,
        Deeply rooted in the ground.
    A huge, strong tree,
        With branches reaching the loftiest heights,
        With roots extending to their furthest depths.
    A curious, enthusiastic traveler,
        Who never stops exploring and searching,
        Who constantly tours uncharted territories.
    A mix of all primal elements,
        The fire of passion, the air of intelligence,
        The water of creativity, the earth of stability.
You are my God-gifted vessel,
        In which I expand and grow,
        Beyond bounds and limits.
You are my mirror and window,
        Through which I get to see,
        My majestic self.

Riding the Waves of Bliss

He is sitting on a large pillow
over a beautiful Indian-designed sheet
in a lotus position, with his woman

sitting in his lap, her legs wrapped around
his waist, chest to chest firmly pressing
together, arms hugging each other tightly,

eyes closed through the end,
mouths kissing in mutual resuscitation;
he is inside of her warm chamber,

both moving up and down,
in a pelvic rocking movement,
like a rhythmic Tantric dance,

creating erotic stimulation inside each other and
powerful streams of energy through the genitals
upward through their spines to their mouths,

generating infinite circular flow passing through
her body to his body, causing a wonderful rush of
sensations all over their joint body, of feelings of

letting go, surrendering, becoming one,
riding the waves of bliss, in an undulating motion,
continuing their journey to ecstasy beyond nirvana,

where duality and separation evanesce, where
boundaries of the physical and spiritual realms vanish,
reaching a unity of all polarities,

male and female, positive and negative,
giver and taker, inner and outer,
joining their lotus flowers in a circular chain

of lighting, merging into a single blossom crowning
their heads, feeling the divine rapture,
seeing the light of their souls in unison.

The Sculpture and the Lover

A large art studio basement,
revolving metal and wooden stools,
huge plastic garbage cans,

unfinished sculptures of clay,
cluttered along the walls,
five women working on male figures,

and I, an amateur male bystander,
bringing a female figure to perfection,
turning discarded trash into a beautiful lady.

As a skilled lover,
I began remodeling her to my liking,
discovering her and uncovering

in the unmolded raw clay
with no model to observe.
I know her very well,

the curves of her body,
the indentations of her muscles,
the markings of her femininity.

I see her in my vision
voluptuously lying in a resting
position as I am making love to her

in the heat of the night
softly touching and retouching
her soft skin, playing gently with

her long neck, petting her
thick hair, rubbing her
sensuous breasts, moving down

to her rounded buttocks into
her inner thighs with
wet fingers stroking passionately,

slowly coming to ecstasy,
finishing with blissful joy.
The sculpture is ready.

Streams of Love

The waterfalls gushing down
sweeping forward with full force

through our embracing bodies
downstream meets upstream

confluence of waters
rushing headlong to the open sea

causing the wedding of waters
yours and mine in a mighty union

reaching at last
a state of ecstasy.

I Want to Stay Inside You

I want to anchor in your deep harbor
    And feel the waves of ecstasy sweeping my body terrains.
I want to sink in your divine fountain
    And immerse my total being in its healing waters.
I want to disappear in your vast ocean
    And drift to hidden shores unknown to man.
I want to dissolve in total love
    And be melted by the fire of your carnal desire.
I want to dip into our blended nectar
    And yield to the secrets of our tender hearts.
I want
        to stay
                inside
                      you.

To Kiss You

To kiss you
Is to invite your tongue
To dance the tango with my craving tongue.

To kiss you
Is to drink all of you
As if my cup overflows.

To kiss you
Is to sip together
From the fountain of life.

To kiss you
Is to lose you
Under the spell of your sublime beauty.

To kiss you
Is to become endlessly intoxicated
With the sweet nectar of the union of our lips.

To kiss you
Is to embrace your lips
As a seal of love upon your mouth.

To kiss you
Is to breathe you
In a closed circle.

To kiss you
Is to be a love captive
Within your walls.

Heavenly Union

It happens in the twilight,
    Every Friday late afternoon,
After the sun sets,
    Before the moon appears,
The Holy One departs from the east,
    Garbed in a mantle of light and wreathed in mist.
He is enwrapped in royal majesty and splendor,
    A carpet of lights spread before Him in the heavens high.
Flaming angels chant in his honor,
    "Come, my Beloved, to meet your Bride."
The Shechinah readies herself in the far west,
    Clothed in a light blue gown adorned with stars.
She yearns for the splendor of His face,
    Her heart beats strongly for His coming.
The host of heaven jubilates for them,
    With trumpets and a sound of the shofar,
Closer and closer they approach each other,
    The spirit of holy Sabbath fills the air.
They meet under a bridal canopy,
    Woven by angels with purple colors of sunset.
Seeing Himself in the mirrors of Her eyes,
    He greets Her with a happy smile.
Surrendering to the radiating light of His countenance,
    She gently closes Her eyes.
He passionately embraces her into His heart,
    As a bridegroom rejoices over his bride.

My Perfect Ten

You are the **one** and only –
A cosmic seed
A heavenly bud
Where everything begins
And new life sprouts
For us both.

We make **two** –
Like heaven and earth
In one universe of love
Complementing our opposites
Growing and expanding
Fashioning oneness beyond duality.

You are the source of **three** –
The creator of new life
The bearer of our fruits of love
Birthing out of a wondrous womb
A blend of divine and human
Like you and I.

You are the builder of **four** –
The stable square
That became our home
A sacred space
A meeting place of our tender hearts
Where flames of passion twist and dance.

You are my **five** –
All senses together
Guiding me
Through the inevitable chaos
Of earthly existing
To a safe haven of worldly pleasures.

With you I am **six** –
Able to intermingle spirit and matter
To bring into being
Who I am
A six-pointed star of faith
Your Shield of David.

You are my **seven** heavens –
A huge space for me to grow
A whole planet
Of shapes and colors to see
A vast realm
Of dreams for me to live.

You are my infinite **eight** –
A magic touch
That unifies two living cycles
Spirit to spirit
Flesh to flesh
In a total embrace.

You are my wise **nine** –
The balance in the rhythm of life
That brings the ebb and tide
Of time and space
To a perfect harmony and completion
Day by day, night by night.

You are My Perfect Ten

A Song to My Beloved
(Read to my beloved, Rosie, on our 40th wedding anniversary)

Ever since the look of your eyes ignited
a fire inside my heart
and the merging of our lips splashed
sparks into the innermost space of my world,
my soul has been bound to you.

As a lily among thorns
so were you, my beloved, among the girls.
As a rose among all fragrant flowers
only you, my soul's delight,
have blossomed in my garden.

From all the girls, I vowed to you:
'Behold, you are consecrated to me'
'And I will betroth you with faith'
that you make our tent holy
and the sanctuary of our love the holy of holies.

Indeed, I have loved you, my beloved,
with all my heart, with all my soul, and with all my being.
With the flaming fire of my soul I engraved,
as a sign upon the tablet of my heart, that my love for you
shall never depart from me.

Even in days of sorrow and pain,
when a sea of tears separated us,
I loved you,
and the flames of my desire for you
kept illuminating the darkness of my world.

I knew then, my beloved,
that many waters cannot
quench a true love,
neither can roaring floods drown it,
even in days of trouble.

I have served you, my beloved,
as Jacob served Rachel,
and all those years together seemed to be
but a few days,
for the love I have had for you.

I remember the kindness of your youth,
the love of your bridals,
how you captivatingly went after me,
for forty years,
in the wilderness in a land that was unsown.

I will not forget how your hands
have never ceased watering the soil of our life,
turning desert into paradise
and a single womb into a fertile dwelling,
full of children and grandchildren.

From the very beginning of our travel,
you have been my soul mate,
a fountain that has never dried up,
a precious angel from heaven,
the only princess in my tower.

You are beautiful, my beloved,
none like you among women,
You are altogether delightful,
with value far exceeding that of rubies,
glamorous, as you were on our wedding day.

Come, my beloved, come, my bride,
let me kneel down,
vow to be faithful to you like yesterday,
ask again for your tender hands,
and kiss them before we continue our long journey.

The Kiss of Life

When I am leaving This World
Before my soul departs
Lean your head over mine
Whisper to me softly
"I love you"
And offer my lips
The Kiss of Life
So that with the touch of your lips
I will wake up to a new life
In the World-to-Come
Where I will be waiting for you.

ONENESS and HARMONY

As Above, So Below

In the beginning,
God created the heaven and the earth.

And God caused the heaven
to rain upon the earth
and the earth to bring up the mist.

Set in full harmony,
the heaven above and the earth below
watered each other.

And God created man,
in His image He created him
male and female.

Placed in a complete union
the male above and the female below
saturated each other.

And God saw this blissful conjugation
to be good and fertile,
yielding seeds and producing fruits.

In the end,
man forgot his mission.

He ravages father heaven
and spoils mother earth;
he pillages women
and devastates men.

He explores the space of heaven
instead of curing the ills of earth;
he pays only in money and kind
rather than respect and kindness.

The planet is confused and tangled
and darkness dominates humanity;
The upper world weeps
and the lower world sinks in turmoil.

Unless we act as humankind,
treat the earth as heaven
and dwell in unity again,
We will banish the Spirit of God from its home.

Truth

No such thing as truth.
There is Truth
    as well as many truths.
When your truth
    merges with mine
    like a river joining the vast sea,
    they become one whole,
    the 'whole truth', a universal truth;
Not just yours or mine, but ours,
    all blend together and blossom
    like a petalled rose emerging from one stem
    offering its sweet fragrance and infinite beauty
    to humanity.

Peace

Academicians use me for credit.
Journalists misuse me for story.
Politicians abuse me for power.

I am not an idea
For you to talk about;
I am an ideal
For you to live up to.

I am not the absence of war
For you to pretend;
I am the presence of harmony
For you to maintain.

I am not just a noun,
The final destination;
I am also a verb,
The practice during my life journey.

Yes, I have a dream

Yes, I have a dream
That we will one day live in a shared land
Where people use their arms for hugging
Where the rainbow of peace shines above
And the spirit of love dominates below.

Yes, I have a dream
That we plow our land together
Decorate it with blossoming gardens
So our children smell the flowers
Walk hand in hand to pick the fruits.

Yes, I have a dream

Brothers-in-Arms

Drop all arms, brother,
Give up your tugging
Join hands with the other
Arms are for hugging.

Ignore your warlord's plies
Call to arms he only knows
Listen to your heart's cries
Love it only shows.

Do not keep at arm's length and far
Staying apart from your friend
Show the world who you really are
Our peace to you we extend.

You and I:
A Quadrilogy on Oneness

a. Transcending Separation

you
and   I
are the same
members of the
human commonwealth
of beings invisibly one with
the universe corporeally divided
into separate physical entities anxious
to open up to relationship eager to transcend the
illusion of plurality through metaphorical acts of
oneness in   flesh and   in spirit
we
share common bread and drink from the same cup
in the spirit of brotherhood
we
shake hands in greeting and hold each other in arms
in the spirit of friendship
we
caress our lips together and join in carnal union
in the spirit of love

b. A Flower of Being

you and I
are the same if
you believe the
Lord created us
all human beings
like colored flowers
of different traits to
decorate mother earth
with our beautiful faces

if you are willing to take a look
deep into your heart of compassion
take off the corolla upon your head
and peal off the petals of your ego
leaving yourself truly naked
in your bud of innocence
you will find out
we're the same
you and I

c. A House of Worship

                you
              and I
         are the same
     praying in His house
  with the foundation laid by Moses
with the walls erected by Jesus Christ
with the roof built by Prophet Muhammad
each sharing his own contribution to the oneness of
    God   God
    man   man
    and   and
   faith faith faith faith faith faith faith faith

d. In the Heart of Hearts

you
and   I
are the same
beyond the walls of suspicion that separate us
beyond the barriers of hatred that set us apart
beyond the gulf of bloody conflict
beyond the hostility
there
in the heart of hearts
in the realm of human oneness
in the sphere of spiritual inter-connectedness
in the world of peace, compassion, and empathy
you and I
are the
same

AWAKENING and ILLUMINATION

Transcendental Visions

Cold winds blow with rattling sounds
Menacing to break in
Through an unlocked window.

Misty rain clouds the sky
Dimming the sight of
The far-reaching horizon.

Smoky fog shrouds the surrounding grassland
Forming an obscure haze
Of a spring day.

The inexplicable beauty
Of these transcendental visions
Always captures my soul.

Am I taken to a distant past
When God dwelled on earth
Wrapping everyone with clouds of love?

Am I carried to an unfamiliar land
Where everything blossoms
And life never dies?

Am I visited by a guardian angel
Bringing a deciphered message
That trembles in my heart?

Am I touched by a concealed light
Passing through the gray fog
Of my own bewilderment?

Seeking Illumination

In dark days of stillness and leaves falling,
When everything is cold and gloomy,
It is the opportune time to pause,
To descend deep into the space of darkness,
Where the splendor of my soul is in full glory.

Only when I take shelter in its light,
And cleave to its splendid beauty,
My spirit is saturated with joy,
And my whole world is dazzling
With brilliant illumination.

Discourse of Souls

One thanksgiving night,
After sharing a festive meal
Together with our children.
I fell into a deep sleep
And had an odd dream.

I asked:
"What is the soul all about?"
A voice replied:
"We are all born with garments of imperfection;
The gem of perfection is our soul."

"Speak your soul!"
The voice counseled me.
"But, how would I know if my ego
Is the one to talk?" I wondered.
"What is the soul?" I insisted.

"If you want to know,
Come to me!"
"Where are you," I asked
But received no answer,
Leaving me in sadness.

When I woke up seeing
My beloved at my side
I realized
She was the inner voice
In my dream.

When she shared with me
Her own sad dream
I knew I visited,
By special invitation,
The shrine of her soul.

Noticing the tears in her eyes,
Feeling the wounds in her heart
I embraced her and said:
"I'll take care of you, my love,
This is my thanksgiving gift to you."

Soul Visions

In a moment of solitude and deep meditation,
I once approached my soul, complaining:

"Oh, my soul, you selected my body from all humans
as your own sanctuary to dwell in my house
like a prisoner of love serving a life term
behind impregnable walls without leaving me
the keys to get to know you before you depart."

I cried when I suddenly heard my soul
whispering in my ear: "Indeed, your body is
my house and the third eye beyond the wall of
darkness in the depths of your inner self is the window
to my secret you desire to know; come to me."

After a short journey in the sea of night,
across a deep black hole, I arrived at the seat of
a hidden light, where time and space are
nonexistent and nothing is concealed. There,
I saw visions of my magnificent soul coming up

>   As an ancient lantern
>   Shining light from the inside out
>   Through my transparent flesh and blood.

As a primeval fountain
Linked to one celestial river of related spirits
That flows into the vast ocean of divinity.

As a bird of paradise
Using sacred notes of heavenly inspiration
To chant sounds of wisdom in my ears.

As an eternal flame
Kindling like a torch of blue-in-red fire
Inside the holy of holies of my heart.

The kaleidoscopic exhibit was interrupted
as I heard again my soul
whispering softly to my heart:
"I am that I am – whatever you want me
to be that's what you see."

Always a Child

Always a child
Despite my age,
I'm still a child,
Accepting no limits,
Knowing no fears,
To reach new heights,
Walk on clouds,
Climb the moon,
Fly magic wings,
From heaven to heaven,
Singing my song.

Stages of Life

Every path of man's life
Is predestined by God,
Charted for a purpose
As a stairway of four separate stages,
If you believe, like me,
In cosmic evolution, or the Tree of Life.

        As a child,
I was mischievous,
The notorious imp
Of my neighborhood.
Kids feared me
Grown-ups scolded me
My parents punished me.
My childhood, so they tell,
Was infested with quarrels.

        As a young man,
I was patriotic,
Educated to love the Land
Trained to fight to the death
For a warring nation –
A militant activist
Then, a combat soldier,
A natural progression
For a zealous nationalist.

As a married man,
After two bloody wars,
The study of the enemy,
Its history and culture,
Became the next stage –
A scholar, a military historian
With reputation,
Using the pen
Instead of a gun.

Now, in mid-life,
Making history has become my mission,
Writing the future, rather than
Recounting the past.
Building on life experiences,
God paved the way
For my final role –
A peacemaker with passion
Transforming the hearts of foes.

Out of Jail

A man is born free
So they all claim,
The philosophers who are
Venerated for their wisdom,
Yet forgetting to notice
One tragic phenomenon.

A man goes straight
To the prison of his mind
Locking himself for life
Behind bars of distorted perceptions
Though attempting to break away,
If he realizes he's there.

Even
When he incidentally
Takes off his blinders for a moment
Seeing what is really out there,
He ends up back
In his self-imposed jail.

But
Every time he takes an incursion
Into the space of new possibilities,
It becomes increasingly easier
To unchain
The shackles of old realities.

Always
Experiencing what life has to offer
Fulfilling unrealized dreams
Embracing the world with joy
Without the fear of going back to jail
Is all he wishes.

The Invisible Mirror

For me,
Other people are the mirror
Of the old phenomenon
Called "aging,"
A silent, creeping process
That fortunately grows
Without my attention, but

Lately I realize
This invisible mirror
Plays strange tricks on me,
You see, I used to think
I am young
And everybody else old
(I still do sometimes), but

Now that my children
Are not so young anymore,
I seem to feel old, and everybody else young,
Although my wife is consistently telling me,
At my new age of advanced age,
I am so young and handsome,
(according to her mirror), but

Still I prefer
My own mirror
The one that never speaks
And does the job to remind me
That there are, and will always be,
People older than me
To make me feel young, but

Recently everybody around me
Began to look older,
Including those I know are younger,
And when I saw not long ago
An old picture of mine, where
I did not recognize myself,
I started to question the credibility of my old mirror.

Riding to Nowhere

Another day of riding
the trails of life
on my aged horse

the hot sun hits my back
sweat pours off
my weary face

as I sadly notice
the lengthy furrows
extending endlessly and

the oasis on the far horizon
is just an illusory mirage
that never appears to be closer

The Tree of Life

In my heart, I planted a magnificent garden
to house my burning love, and there,
in this blossoming paradise,
I found a merciful and forgiving God.

I did not stop plowing, sowing,
bowing down, and kneeling,
worshiping Him one furrow after another,
even giving Him sacrifices and offerings.

Now its roots are spreading deep in my heart
feeding fortitude to my trunk of faith
inviting its crowning branches to cover my universe
and its hanging fruits to sweeten my meditation.

What is God?

What is God

If not the attraction to a hidden force
    Whose mystery has not been resolved;
Or, the longing for a lost paradise
    Where man is draped with eternal light;
Or, the yearning for unity
    Which leads to redemption and liberation;
Or, the powerful aspiration for perfection
    For which people are ready to die;
Or, perhaps the source of love
    Whose power is as strong as the flame of fire;
Or, the ideal image of beauty
    That carries no blemish at all.

God is maybe all of the above
Created by human reverence and awe.

Where are You, God?

Ever since You drove me out of the Garden of Eden
To till the ground on Planet Earth
And settled the cherubim at Your gates
The flame of their swords keeps me away from You.

    Where are You, God?
We banished You into exile
Expelled You into our own sanctuaries
Far away from our real life on Earth
Not knowing how to bring You back.

    Where are You, God?
I call You with numerous Names
But I do not hear You.
I study your Holy Book
But I cannot find You.

    Where are You, God?
Am I destined to see You only upon my death?
Can't You teach me how to know You during my lifetime?
Where can I see Your hidden face?
Have You forgotten me?

Where are You, God?
Will You answer me?
Will You help me notice Your voice?
How do I find You?
Can You come closer so I can touch You?

Where are You, God?

Our Life

Our life -
a
long
narrow
bridge
across the great River Time.

Our days -
just
a
short
passage
from an uncertain future to a vanished past.

Our world -
much
work
to
do
between This World and the World-to-Come.

Direct Line to Heaven

Abraham
In mid-day
Sat on his stool meditating
At the entrance of his tent
Looked at the horizon
And saw
The angels of peace coming

Isaac
In the afternoon
Went out barefoot to nearby meadow
Heard the trees moaning
Smelled the flowers' fragrance
And listened to the birds
Singing halleluiah

Jacob
In the late evening
Placed his head
On a hard rock
Closed his eyes
And climbed his ladder
To meet the Creator

So do I,
See my heart
A temple without walls
A sanctuary wide open
A private holy of holies
Where God and I
come together.

Everyone has a direct line to heaven

God Must Have Had a Plan

God destroyed Sodom and Gomorrah,
Two cities filled with wickedness,
But saved Lot,
Who, under the influence of the drink,
Slept with his seductive daughters
Who bore them two sons,
Moab and Ammon,
Later to be great nations.

Thus far the prelude.

Then, centuries later, Ruth,
A faithful Moabite widow,
A princess, they say,
Who desired to convert,
Fell for Boaz,
A distinguished chief
In the neighboring land of Judah,
Bore him children.
And became the ancestress of King David
A fifth generation far removed.

And what followed
Is an esteemed dynasty,
Strangely descended from gentiles
Born out of incest,
Becoming the revered House of David,
Which we hope
To rebuild into,
The line of the future Messiah,
The promised deliverer,
Whose coming we all pray for.

God must have had a plan.

On the Top of Mount God

Revelations have occurred on mountains:
On Mount Sinai, Moses received God's revelation.
Then, In Galilee, Jesus delivered the Sermon on the Mount.
Muhammad followed with his last sermon on Mount Arafat.

So did I, in my dream,
Climb Mount God, so called Har-El,
To face the Almighty
And enter the abode of the Immortals.

Like a spiritual mountaineer,
Unafraid of the perils of the ascent,
I made the journey alone
Seeking illumination and revelation.

The summit in the far distance
Was covered by white blankets of snow
And draped by swirling cloud formations,
Signs of greatness and awe.

As I approached the windy mountain peak,
Crossing into the borderland between
The physical and heavenly realms,
I noticed the scenery of my inner self.

Against the background of
The vast garments of the world
Seen from the mountaintop,
My human existence seemed miniscule.

The dichotomy between
The lofty rock of divinity and
The underlying valley of human vanity
Was a perfect place to test the fortitude of my faith.

At night, on top of the holy mount,
I laid down under the vast canopy of heaven
Covered myself with overlays of fluffy clouds
And fell asleep.

In my dream inside the dream,
I watched my own climbing of Jacob's Ladder,
The mystic staircase to the celestial,
Accompanied by winged angels with human faces.

After a series of internal contentions
Between my resistant flesh and my overpowering spirit
A miraculous disembodiment took place
As I entered with exhilaration into a veritable paradise.

When I woke up in an early morning hour,
I wondered how Moses, Jesus, and Muhammad
Made the difficult return away from the Light of God
Back to the undesirable realm of earthly existence.

DEATH and GRIEVING

A Hidden Visitor

You must have invaded my body
a long time ago, planting a malignant
seed inside me, believing you have
some genetic rights over my life.

> Did you always believe
> Planting your seed inside me,
> That you had genetic rights to my life?

You have been an unwelcome guest,
who had drunk from the hand of the devil
the cup of his venom and then
came in to devour my flesh.

> You've been most unwelcome,
> Drinking from the devil's cup
> As you wash down my flesh.

You have been a hidden visitor,
who has been growing freely like a parasite,
sucking the juice of my vitality
without my knowledge.

> You've been a parasitic visitor,
> Sucking the juice
> Of my vitality.

But now that I know,
I hereby cut you off,
sever our ties of blood,
release you forever.

You must die so that I can live.

My Funeral Cry

It must be painful to hear
    The heartbreaking news I fear
That my Dad may suddenly die
    Without saying good bye.

Isn't this burial event
    People had to invent
For children to honor their dead
    Made to serve the living instead?

It is truly my funeral cry
    I don't want to deny
Not to experience how life does not last
    Not to learn how human existence is past.

It is my own sense of precipice
    I don't want to miss
Not to feel the chill of my individual mortality
    Not to mourn my own fatality.

Three Goddesses of Destiny

Three goddesses decree the destiny of man.
Three goddesses rule over all flesh and blood.

One weaves the wick of life
spinning the spindle and moaning.

The second makes the final judgment
who shall live and who shall be bound to the alter.

The third one cuts the wick
bowing down her head in dignified silence.

Each of them fulfill a role
together they make a whole.

Thus, there is no way out of death
no chance at all to find refuge.

Visiting the Cemetery

A few things have changed since
My last visit in the city cemetery.
The dead reside there crowded without complaining,
Rich along with poor, righteous with wicked,
All together under one heavenly roof.

Like it is in any egalitarian society,
No grave site is spared
By the visit of friendly pigeons
Who leave their droppings
On every tombstone.

When I am there, I perform the customary ritual
Of washing the marble gravestones
Of my deceased father and brother,
Place some gravel over the cleaned surface
And wait for next year.

Until then, the pigeons will pay their visit.

To Life or Death

When a man is born he begins to die.
It is only a matter of time and measure.
      Like the steady rhythm of an hour glass
          His days diminish without ticking or noise.
One morning he gets up and never returns
And nothing in the world helps.
      Only God in heaven knows
          Whom to keep alive and whom to cut off.
It is a question of fate that was decreed
By the hand of God Who is strong and swift.
      Imagine you could request of Him
          To foresee death.
Surely, the world will never stop crying
And man will only appeal and protest.
      Therefore, it's impossible to postpone a heavenly verdict
          Only to hope we have the strength to wake up;
To protect our body and spirit
And to believe in Divine Providence.

Life after death

For seven days
They kept coming one after another
To give respect to my deceased father
And offer condolences to the mourners.
My father's life has passed in procession
In a long parade of faces and images
An endless chain of representatives
From a close and distant past.
Isn't this show distasteful
To watch a man's life
Displayed publicly
Only upon his death?
Now that the mourning is over
And people stopped coming,
Until the next death
God knows whose.

I am a Holocaust Survivor
*(Dedicated to Clara, my mother-in-law,
who survived the Holocaust)*

The forces of evil
Killed my family
Wounded my heart
Violated my innocence
Robbed my youth
Crushed my dreams
Left me behind alive and dead.

Fed by an overflowing spring of tears
Plagued by mutilated visions
Of violence and humiliation
I have locked myself inside
My own built-in concentration camp
Surrounded by self-made barbed wires
So nobody could have access to me.

I still refuse to accept liberation
To insure that no peace is allowed
And as long as I am alive
I will hold on to my misery so that
You feel sorry for my never-ending torment
Know evil has never disappeared
And good is not worth appreciating.

I will not surrender to my heart
That is still bleeding
Longing for the past
Where I belong
With other forgotten multitudes
In the ruined graveyards
Of my vanished hometown.

Elegy to Shmulik
*(Dedicated to my deceased brother,
and read in the 30th day of Unveiling the Stone)*

Suddenly, in one bright day,
I was shaken by roaring thunder,
You perished without warning
I was left broken and enraged.

You walked away from us to rest
In a world that is all good,
You left us in grief
In a bed of tears and wet pillows.

You should know, dear brother,
That you shined upon my way with your death,
My world is getting empty here
Without our country you so praised.

But how can I return for good
To build there a home,
Without seeing you even for a moment
Or to get away together for an outing?

How can I recite chants
On Friday nights,
Without your outshining face,
With no personal conversation?

Perhaps my words have dried out
But not the tears,
And certainly not the accordion music
You have voiced in my ears for hours.

I am saying good-by
Till the next meeting,
Maybe in the dream
Where the commotion is so heavy.

As in every generation
We will reach you one day,
Leave the earthly vestibule
Shout out together in the divine parlor.

Mother, Don't Cry

Nobody but I understands your sorrow
Grieving alone in your home
Memories anguish the heart
Leaving no cure for the pain.

    Mother, don't cry
The angels guard Dad
They sow a coat of stripes for Shmulik
For their well-being they care
That's the custom in the World of Truth.

    Mother, don't cry
I have no explanation
Why they lie down in the grave
Under a cover of soil and stone
Wrapped in white linen.

    Mother, don't cry
Their candle has never been extinguished
They only passed into the World-to-Come
Life there is fundamentally so different
Without a body, with no flesh and blood.

Mother, don't cry
They are also with us here on earth
Their souls warm our hearts
Wherever we go or turn
We'll watch the traces of their spirits.

Mother, don't cry

Change of Address

The angel of death visited us twice.
When it took away my father's soul
We thought his death was from heaven
And an inquiry would only cause pain.

But, when he chose to kill my brother
Immediately at the mourning's anniversary
We exposed the act of deception
The source of evil and a curse.

A delegation of wicked angels
Found an easy address
To learn their profession
And also to ridicule a crying family.

But before they paid another visit
We turned to the post office of our Acclaimed God
And also performed an Additional Prayer for Him
Asking to change the cursed zip-code.

A Wandering Spirit

Another wandering spirit
is crying in heaven above
loudly weeping
wherever she goes.

Many long years
she sustained a living creature
so how can she not lament deeply
over the loss of her human body.

But the nature of a spirit
after the heart stops
is to find consolation
inside a newborn.

She is always passing
like a torch from one hand to another
into a new body she is entering
keeping a transient life.

But, our lot is grief and pain
engaging in a formal mourning
digging another grave
for a spiritless body.

Nightmare

Slowly and sluggishly,
I am going down the stairs
And there you are, calling
"Why are you here?"

You notice me
And wave your hand.
Does it mean I'm also dead
Or is it just a dream?

I ignore you
Because I'm alive and you're dead
And why should I respond to you
If this is not truly happening?

I am entering into a public urinal
And there is my deceased father
Pulling down his pants
And comfortably urinating.

"Did you see your son?" I asked,
"What is he doing here
Together with you and your kind?
Do you live here in the same place?"

"And what brings you here?"
Asked my father with no hesitation
"You don't belong to our community,"
And I suddenly woke up.

At that restless night
I fell asleep
Yet kept one eye open
Making sure I didn't find myself dead.

Death of a Flower

A tender and fresh flower
Too young to be cut off
Should only be stroked
As our gardening teacher taught.

But you, my brother,
Your life was cut off abruptly
Plucked with rage and haste
God's hand was responsible for your decimation.

I do not have the answer, my dear,
Why beautiful flowers and good people die
Along with thorny thistles and evildoers.
God is not my acquaintance.

Maybe you were planted in our heavenly court
Among the flowers of Paradise
Where your soul is saturated with sacred waters
And your garden is filled with everything that is good.

But here on earth
Our garden is flooded with endless tears
For the anguish of loss and destruction
For the calamity God inflicted upon us.

Every Person Finds for Himself a Flower

The cyclamen dwells on rocky cliffs
Hiding from strangers
Bowing her head
Shy and conciliatory.

From all the beautiful flowers of the land
You truly loved her
During long and weary trips
You devotedly looked after her.

Since every person finds for himself in nature
A flower that resembles his character
He will search for it everywhere
For it is full of beauty.

Therefore your grave is wrapped
With greenery Cyclamens all around
A sign for the beginning of a chapter
A harbinger of an approaching spring.

On My Tombstone

I.

When I die one day
Say no eulogies and lamentations
For the loss of a wholesome man
No praises for a man of wisdom.

Make your heart happy and your spirit rejoice
For a man who enjoyed plenty,
Did exceedingly well,
Knew how to give and also to take.

Remember me as I have been
From infancy to adulthood,
How I have truly lived
From the cradle to the grave.

And if you still insist on engraving
Some unusual words on my stone,
Please write:
"Here lies the oldest man ever lived."

II.

My dad died
and then my brother died.
and now I am dying

to live with my back facing backward,
far from the valley of darkness,
straight into a shining future

yet to be born,
where I will chisel
the tombstone of my life

using the flame of my passion
for engraving the essence
of what my life is all about:

"And after all
that was said and done,
he was, he is and he shall be."

EPILOGUE

I am a Poet

A kabbalist
Seeing the universe as a playground
Filled with letters and colors all around.

A writer
Ornamenting forms of expression
With pearls of artistic impression.

A mystic
Using sacred mantras as a vehicle
Of magic, energy and miracle.

A lover
Joining verses of discourse
As an intimate act of intercourse.

A poet

About the Author

Dr. Shai Har-El is a historian, writer, poet, educator, rabbi, activist, and businessman. He was born in Israel, where he spent his formative childhood and young adulthood. Spending most of his time in the U.S., he manages there his full-service, Illinois-based, financial consulting firm, Har-El Financial Group (see *www.HarelFinancial.com*), and runs the nonprofit, ambitious, private diplomacy organization, Middle East Peace Network (MEPN) (see *www.MEPNetwork.org*). He also gives lectures and workshops, and writes essays on Middle East affairs.

Har-El earned his B.A. and M.A. degrees in Middle Eastern History from Tel Aviv University, and his Ph.D. from the University of Chicago, where he currently serves as an Associate Member of the Center for Middle Eastern Studies (CMES). (For his CV, see *https://cmes.uchicago.edu/content/associate-members*.)

Har-El is the author of the following history textbooks:

Struggle for Domination in the Middle East: The Ottoman-Mamluk War, 1485-1491 (Leiden: E.J. Brill, 1995); *Where Islam and Judaism Join Together: A Perspective on Reconciliation* (New York: Palgrave McMillan, 2014); and *In Search for Israeli-Palestinian Peace: An Urgent Call for a New Approach to Middle East Peace* (New York: Palgrave Macmillan, 2016). His last two books are the fruits of his peace advocacy and activism under MEPN.

Har-El was ordained as a rabbi. He has been running workshops and writing on a variety of religious themes, particularly on the interface between spirituality and personal growth. His forthcoming spiritual self-help book, *Discover the Jewel of Wisdom: Eight Paths to Powerful Living*, is a "living laboratory" report of his own personal findings while plowing the "fields" of life and his spiritual journey toward rabbinic ordination. His anthology, *Many Ways to Courting God: Selected Spiritual Writings*, and meditation guide, *Daily Spiritual Affirmations for Powerful Living*, were assembled as companion books.

Har-El's poetry book, *Riding the Waves of Bliss: Seasons of Life Poems*, which you have just read, is an insight into the changing seasons of his life.

Har-El has lived with his wife, Rosalie of blessed memory, in Highland Park, Illinois, for thirty-four years. He has three children living in the U.S. and Israel, and eleven grandchildren ranging from twelve to twenty three years old.

Contact the author directly at *Shaiharel@comcast.net*

www.ingramcontent.com/pod-product-compliance
Lightning Source LLC
Chambersburg PA
CBHW030332100526
44592CB00010B/662